# Where That Leaves Us

# Where That Leaves Us

*Poems by*

Michael P. Hill

© 2024 Michael P. Hill. All rights reserved.
This material may not be reproduced in any form, published,
reprinted, recorded, performed, broadcast,
rewritten, or redistributed without
the explicit permission of Michael P. Hill.
All such actions are strictly prohibited by law.


Cover photo by Ken Jones
(Special thanks to Chuck Jones for facilitating access. For more of
Ken's work, visit *drkenjones.com*.)
Image preparation by Andrew Hill
Author photo by Sawyer Hill


ISBN: 978-1-63980-583-9

Kelsay Books
502 South 1040 East, A-119
American Fork, Utah 84003
Kelsaybooks.com

For the women who encouraged me and made me a better writer:
*Pat Rapson, Paula Felps & Kathie Hinnen*

# Acknowledgments

Some of the poems in this collection have appeared or are forthcoming in the following publications and exhibitions, sometimes in slightly different forms:

*Appalachian Review:* "Garage Sale"
*Atlanta Review:* "Intermezzo"
*Barstow & Grand:* "Everything Must Go"
*Beach Combings:* "Starfishing"
*Gray's Sporting Journal:* "Small Trout Rising to Bugs in a Stream Near Monet's Gardens, Giverny, France"
*Humana Obscura:* "Burn Scar"
*Jelly Bucket:* "Evening Hatch"
*The Main Street Rag:* "My Great Uncle's Art Studio"
*Memoir Mixtapes:* "Listening to Springsteen"
*Nassau Review:* "Last Call"
*Stillwater Poetry Review:* "Wave"
*Stonecrop Magazine:* "Landfill"
*Talking River Review:* "Teardown," "Two Joggers"
*Valparaiso Poetry Review:* "Ghost Sign"
*Windsor Art & Heritage Center (A Sense of Nostalgia: Exploring the Past):* "Battle of the Bands"

# Contents

Side *A*

| | |
|---|---|
| *Garage Sale* | 15 |
| *Burn Scar* | 16 |
| *Wave* | 17 |
| *Ghost Sign* | 18 |
| *My Great Uncle's Art Studio* | 19 |
| *Last Call* | 20 |
| *Starfishing* | 21 |
| *Landfill* | 22 |
| *Everything Must Go* | 23 |
| *Ascension* | 24 |
| *Teardown* | 25 |
| *Leaf Globe* | 26 |
| *Pompeii* | 27 |
| *Phantom Ligament* | 28 |
| *Halogen* | 29 |
| *Two Joggers* | 30 |
| *Expiration Dates* | 31 |
| *My Daughter, Driving at Night* | 32 |
| *Magi* | 33 |
| *Root Canal* | 34 |
| *Inland Atlantis* | 35 |
| *Battle of the Bands* | 36 |
| *Castaway* | 37 |
| *Small Trout Rising to Bugs in a Stream Near Monet's Gardens, Giverny, France* | 38 |
| *Ghost of a Moon* | 39 |

Side *B*

| | |
|---|---:|
| *Intermezzo* | 43 |
| *Visiting the House I Grew Up In* | 44 |
| *Solar Farm* | 45 |
| *Veteran's Day* | 46 |
| *The Skin-and-Bones Gazette* | 47 |
| *At the Grave of Georges Méliès, Paris, France* | 48 |
| *Breaking Strength* | 49 |
| *Almost Autumn* | 50 |
| *Étude for Solo Cello* | 51 |
| *A Deck of Cards* | 52 |
| *Grand Opening* | 53 |
| *Listening to Springsteen* | 54 |
| *Flag* | 55 |
| *Creation Story* | 56 |
| *Bicycle in the Snow* | 57 |
| *Childish Things* | 58 |
| *Reading in Bed* | 59 |
| *Dandelions* | 60 |
| *"Away We Go"* | 61 |
| *Snow Shuffle* | 62 |
| *Dry Streambed* | 63 |
| *At the Botanic Gardens* | 64 |
| *The Skull* | 65 |
| *Evening Hatch* | 66 |
| *Dead Air* | 67 |

*. . . all this steel and these stories, they drift away to rust . . .*
—Bruce Springsteen

# Side *A*

## *Garage Sale*

Up early on a Saturday,
a flock of local bargain combers
has descended on the house next door,
where tables, washed up by the tide
of departure, are out in the driveway,
spilling over with domestic debris.

In silence they sift through the echoes
of those who made their home here,
their leavings littering this concrete shore
like so many seashells, some chipped,
others cracked, and all of them empty
save for the sound of the ocean.

## *Burn Scar*

Even in full sun,
the bare, beleaguered aspens
here beside the river
appear as silhouettes,

the effect largely owing
to charred husks of bark
slung like tattered overcoats
over their skeletal frames.

And beyond them, more still,
extending up the ridge,
a dreary, defeated regiment
on the long march home,

the odd slash of white
like that of bandaged wounds,
some so deeply felt
they may never heal entirely.

## *Wave*

On the morning
that he set out from Colorado,
I went to hug my firstborn,
who was going away to college
by the ocean and, at once,
a mighty swell rose up
off the coast of California
and came crashing inland, all the way
across a third of the continent,
on a collision course with me,
the sheer force of it owing, I suppose,
to pride, love, excitement
and a sudden, overwhelming sadness
that nearly swept me under,
flooding my eyes as it hit me how,
the entire time, everything
was cresting to this moment,
when the world would come rushing in
and claim him as its own.

## *Ghost Sign*

On the side of an old building
in the middle of downtown,
a spectral Owl Cigar advert
from another century is taking
its own sweet time to disappear,
those once-bright colors receding
into the rust-red brick of the past,
where its claim of "now 5 cents"
means exactly what it says
and its logo perches patiently,
peering out through the years,
all the way to the present, where
it assumes its phantom form.

## *My Great Uncle's Art Studio*

The light in that grand cathedral
of childhood came streaming
through floor-to-ceiling windows

and adhered in sparkling fashion
to the lenses of magnifying glasses
dangling from above, each one

suspended strategically for detail work
before a large, unfinished painting
perched on an easel in the middle

of the room. Near at hand, brushes
beckoned amidst a loose assortment
of misshapen oil color tubes, while

small-scale Masonite studies mingled
with fully realized, framed canvases
and a makeshift magic lantern sat

draped in shadow by the wall, ready
to project images for tracing, which
I guess is what I'm doing now, just

with words, not pencil, the scene
illuminated anew before me as
the memory of it comes beaming

back across the years, straight into
this crowded workspace of my own,
the one up here in my head.

# *Last Call*

> *The removal of the payphone, located at 745 7th Ave., does mark the end of an era of coin-operated communication in New York City.*
> —Gothamist.com, May 23, 2022

I'd hardly more than glanced at the news of the last payphone in New York City being removed and retired to a museum when, old softie that I am, my heart sank like a quarter to the bottom of a coin chute. And as it lay there in the dark, listening, someone outside began murmuring indistinctly into the receiver, rolling the armored cord between their fingers as they leaned the weight of their body against the side of the enclosure, their voice rising and falling and rising and falling some more until at last it fell silent and they brought the handset down on the cradle with a thudding finality, turned on their heel and set off down the sidewalk, never to return.

## *Starfishing*

The moon is out
on the murky river of night

once again, stalking
the shaded banks

with a constellation
for a fly rod, sparkling

celestial bodies
strung along the length of it.

## *Landfill*

A long way from the ocean,
Colorado to be more precise,
a mass of gulls, white as the froth
on the salty, swelling Pacific,

is wheeling above this rolling sea
of castoff possessions, yard waste
and garbage like it was a day
at the beach. Below them, machines

are kicking up sprays of debris
as they rearrange the landscape
into crudely-constructed castles
while dump goers toss trash bags

about as though they were beach balls
and rumbles of afternoon thunder
come rippling over the mountains
like the sound of crashing waves.

## *Everything Must Go*

They've taken down the letters
from the shuttered J.C. Penney
on the south side of town, leaving

dusky, sun-scribed impressions
of what was there before,
the effect being that of fossils

stamped on an ancient riverbed,
and here with a steady stream
of traffic flowing past. Then again,

perhaps it's akin to a painting
discovered behind another painting,
a shadowy presence languishing

in obscurity all these years, only
to finally be brought to light now,
after the artist's demise.

## *Ascension*

On the inside of the door
to our downstairs storage closet,
pencil marks chronicle
the upward progress of my kids
(both of whom are as tall now
as they're likely going to get),
recalling the hieroglyphics
found on the walls of tombs,
detailing deeds in exchange
for safe passage to the afterlife.

And should, millennia from now,
archaeologists discover
the jottings collected here,
I'd like to think that they might
be similarly afforded a glimpse
into the workings of a civilization,
long vanished, where individuals
grew taller and then taller still,
until, as it may be assumed,
they arrived at some higher purpose.

## *Teardown*

Out for a walk with my dogs
on an early spring Saturday morning,
we passed what was left of a house,
freshly demolished, presumably

to clear the site for a new one.
And of that forsaken structure, only
the topmost floor, with its arched gables
and steeply sloped roof, remained,

the ground rising up to meet it as though
the entire dwelling was sinking,
story by story, room by room,
out of the here and now

and into the past, along with
whoever considered it home,
too deep in the day-to-day to detect
their world giving way beneath them.

## *Leaf Globe*

To sit in our many-windowed front room
on a bright and blustery October day
is to have your world turned upside down,
given a good shake, and then set back
upright again, the whole thing swirling
with fallen gold and you there at the center,
content, with nothing better to do but watch.

## *Pompeii*

Among our fellow tourists
in the sweltering Mediterranean,
we set out into the streets
of that city of the disappeared,
Vesuvius looming darkly
as we traced the dusty footpaths
of its long-vanished inhabitants,
wandering through their homes,
their temples and their baths,
all submerged, rooftop-deep,
in ash and pumice centuries ago.

As well-preserved as it was,
from the statues to the columns
to the frescoes to the mosaics,
the presence of the Pompeiians
was palpable, such that we pondered
the things they might've been doing
or thinking on that fateful day
before so many were stilled—
like the plaster casts of bodies
we saw in the Garden of the Fugitives—
by the merciless volcanic tide.

Moreover, the pots and pans
left atop cooking surfaces
and the bread discovered in ovens
evoked a sense of the quotidian,
as though their existence was not
so dissimilar to our own, what with
our routines and our rituals
and our largely unquestioning faith
in the workings of the world,
assuming, as I suppose we must,
that everything will turn out fine.

## *Phantom Ligament*

Owing to a certain skiing mishap,
my wife counts a cadaver's ACL
among her inner workings, relying

on a donation from the deceased
to operate the complex machinery
of her knee, which, at the moment,

is bending to the task of helping her
return someone's serve here tonight
on this floodlit outdoor tennis court,

where, with everything hinging
on the generosity of a stranger,
she moves with the grace of a ghost.

## *Halogen*

Don't get me wrong.
I'm all for cleaner and brighter,
but I'd be lying if I told you
that I didn't lament the loss
of that shining-example-turned-outlaw,
the incandescent light bulb,
whose power to warm up a room
made it easy to see past its shortcomings:
the delicate tungsten filament,
the lack of longevity, even
the risk of it starting a fire. And yet,
it's not as though I'm in the dark
as to why the torch has been passed
to those long-lasting, safe LEDs.
It's just that their harsh efficiency
has a way of leaving me cold
and nostalgic for their predecessors,
ubiquitous once, now all but burnt out
like a last cigarette or a sunset
smoldering there in the distance
beyond the darkening trees.

## *Two Joggers*

Side by side,
this curious pair

makes its singular way
down our city street,

one facing forward
and the other turned around,

trotting in reverse,
such that together

they invoke the impression
of a solitary creature

with a peculiar knack
for seeing what's ahead

while simultaneously
observing where it's been,

four feet pointing
in two different directions

and all of them bearing it
into the future

at once.

## *Expiration Dates*

Sunk deep in shadow
at the back of the pantry
is an oft-neglected graveyard
where good consumables
go to die. Lined up there
like a solemn row of headstones
among the more recently purchased,
each has a story to tell, a lifespan
spelled out like an epitaph,
if only someone would read it.

## *My Daughter, Driving at Night*

Grasping the wheel firmly,
she steers us down the lamplit streets
of our neighborhood, sitting up straight
as she thoughtfully navigates each turn,
switching on her blinker well ahead of time
and taking care to stay in her own lane.
Armed with a freshly minted learner's permit,
there's no slouching, no one-hand-draped-
lazily-atop-the-wheel, nor any of
the other bad habits that that those of us
who've been doing this for a while
invariably seem to pick up. Her confidence
increasing, she accepts my challenge
to take a spin down the main drag, lights
and people suddenly swimming before her
like unfamiliar marine life. Meanwhile,
I help her keep watch for pedestrians
and cars backing out of their spots, parked here
in the passenger seat and trying, like her,
to get used to this strange new arrangement.

# *Magi*

Here among my kingdom of leaves
on a warm day in early November,
I pause from raking to glance over

at the house across the street,
where three men are busy stringing
Christmas lights about the roof.

With Halloween hardly behind us,
Yuletide still seems distant, and yet
here they are, these three, who,

judging by their shabby work van,
have traveled from afar, bearing gifts
of gold, frankincense and myrrh.

## *Root Canal*

You hardly have to know
what such a procedure entails
to experience the particular discomfort
of those two adjacent words.

They certainly don't suggest
any sort of convenient conduit,
pleasant diversion, shortcut
or untroubled passage, not collectively.

In fact, when my wife informed me
of the demise of one of her teeth
and the swift necessity of
this notorious treatment sequence,

I felt a sudden stab of pain
emanate from the nerve endings
in my own mouth, or at least
I imagined I did, sensitive as I am

to the power of language, which,
when harnessed effectively,
has been known to foment revolutions,
upend kingdoms, install new Crowns.

## *Inland Atlantis*

Beneath the reservoir
on the west side of our city
lies the waterlogged ghost town
of Stout, Colorado, its residents
having cleared out by the late forties
on orders from the Bureau of Reclamation,
which flooded it right off the map.

Already on the decline,
there wasn't that much left of it
by the time its fate was sealed; and yet
it endures, spilling beyond its borders
to saturate our collective imagination,
where its small but singular voice
refuses to be drowned out.

## *Battle of the Bands*

More like the British Invasion
than Antietam or Iwo Jima,
we mobilized nevertheless,

separately banding together
in high school auditoriums
and supermarket parking lots

atop flatbed trailers, where
guitarists fought to be heard
above a bombardment of drums

and bass players held the line,
leaving lead singers to clash
with insufficient PA systems,

so much of their wailing in vain.
And after the struggle subsided,
the air still redolent of smoke

from a mortally wounded amplifier,
the battle weary sprawled amid
the rubble of instrument cases,

waiting on word from the front
as to which of those among them
had ultimately prevailed.

## *Castaway*

I'm stretching to go for a run
while my mom looks on from her chair.
It's been either a living room recliner
or a straight-backed one in the kitchen
since she stopped being able to walk,
at least not without a walker, and then
not very far or fast.
                       Her doctors,
with all of their tests, can't explain it;
and my dad, despite his assistance,
can't make her feel any less alone,
not there on her little desert island,
where she sits and watches for ships,
waiting for one to pass close enough
to notice her waving from shore.

## *Small Trout Rising to Bugs in a Stream Near Monet's Gardens, Giverny, France*

One can only assume
it has no idea of the context
in which it is doing about the most natural thing
for a trout to be doing, nor any inkling

as to why all these eager tourists
keep on crossing this little footbridge
just upstream of where it is going to town,
devouring newly hatched insects

without a care in the world, and, more than likely,
without any appreciation for the world famous
water lily pond next door, Claude Monet,
the Impressionists, or even art in general.

It's just hungry. Or acting on instinct. Whatever.
The point is, it's putting on quite a show
for me in this showy little Eden
where the great French painter cultivated

inspiration for himself until his death
in 1926 and, despite everything I should be
concentrating on here, I can't help but wonder
what I might be able to do with a fly rod about now.

## *Ghost of a Moon*

A chalky smudge appearing
on a powder blue afternoon sky,
it slowly accumulates shadows,
advancing from mere suggestion
to full-blown apparition with
the dying of the day, en route
to its nightly perch on high,
where it turns its haunted gaze
on the darkly veiled world below.

# Side *B*

## *Intermezzo*

It's a weekday afternoon
on a quiet street, precious little
moving but for the breeze
when, all at once, a garbage truck
lurches onto the scene, roaring
up the block, two sanitation workers
hanging off the back. As it turns
down an alley, there's a sharp whiff
of music, a pop tune blasting
from the rig and, just like that,
the trash men are transformed
into song-and-dance men, singing,
along with Lorde, about how they too
will "never be royals," before vanishing,
first from sight and then from earshot,
into the rest of the day, almost
like nothing ever happened.

## *Visiting the House I Grew Up In*

Because we were in the neighborhood
and because it had been a decade
or more since we'd seen the old place,
my kids and I turned in the driveway
and followed the familiar crunch
of the gravel on up to the porch.
And there, we encountered a stranger, who,
upon learning who we were,
invited the three of us in for what
amounted, I guess, to a tour
of my childhood, which we began
by squeezing into the mud room, where
my dog once delivered a litter
of nine ebony pups. From there,
we passed through the low-ceilinged kitchen,
site of my fledgling forays into
French toast and chocolate chip cookies, then
ascended the narrow staircase and
traversed the close-quartered hallway,
concluding high in the attic, where
my dad's old model railroad table
crouched in amongst the shadows.
In essence, then, much was the same.
It was just that everything was smaller
than how I'd remembered it, which
can leave you feeling sort of like
an unexpected visitor on
the doorstep of your life, stealing
a glance in the rearview mirror as
whoever you might have been
shrinks into the distance.

## *Solar Farm*

Down in the Valley of Fire,
where the red sandstone rises
up from the floor of the Mojave,

a sight all too easily mistaken
for a mirage by interstate travelers
comes flitting concretely into view:

row upon row of black glass panels
shimmering with a blazing harvest
of desert sun. Stretching on, as far

as the eye can see, they undulate
like darkly luminous leaves rooted
improbably in sheer desolation

as they bathe in the fierce glow
of what passes for irrigation here,
flourishing to brilliant effect.

# *Veteran's Day*

In my neighbor's front yard,
an embattled locust tree
stands in stark contrast
to a peacetime autumn sky,
barren but for a few seed pods
dangling from its branches
like rusty, old combat medals.

Its limbs all pruned back
to try to keep the end at bay,
it has taken on the appearance
of an elderly amputee soldier,
extending itself upward
with everything it has left
in something resembling a salute.

## *The Skin-and-Bones Gazette*

I'm a little worried about the newspaper.
Okay, more than a little. I mean, look at it—

it's wasting away to nothing. And this
despite the fact there's no shortage

of news out there these days, no lack
of front-page headline fodder, opinions

or even gossip column material to nourish it
back to health, maybe fatten it up a little.

And if that weren't enough, the advertising
is giving it a run for its money, dead set,

it appears, on reducing it to an also-ran,
a has-been, a scrawny, ink-smudged shadow

of its former self, not so much information-filled
as information-deprived, scant on scoops

and not good for much of anything anymore
but cleaning windows or lining the cat box.

# *At the Grave of Georges Méliès, Paris, France*

*French filmmaker and illusionist, 1861–1938*

Your particular magic
brought wondrous imaginings
to life before our eyes:

mermaids, giants,
fire-breathing dragons,
even the inhabitants

of the moon. And here,
for your last trick, it seems
you've outdone yourself:

put down your camera,
conjured a puff of smoke
and vanished into the ether.

## *Breaking Strength*

Sitting by the side of the river,
I cinch up the knot connecting
my leader to my fly, pulling it tight
and then giving it a tug or two more
as a test, the act reminding me
of the last time I fished with my son,
who recently went off to college,
and how we've gone fishing together
less and less these past few years, which
I suppose is the way of things, a test
of sorts, a relationship pulled taut,
and now, of course, he's a thousand
miles away and I have to wonder when
we'll ever get back out on the water
again and what things will be like
without him around all the time, when
my rumination is cut short by the grunt
of my smartphone, which I fish out
of the chest pocket of my waders and
glance at, discovering a text message
from my son, whose presence here,
even digital, lifts my heart, compelling me
to stand and step out into the current,
confident something will rise.

## *Almost Autumn*

An orange-pink sun ascends
a tentative, blue-gray sky
as I drive the sleepy back roads
of Wisconsin's Western Upland,

fog lying thick in the hollows
and the mingled scent of earth,
moss and wood smoke lacing
the early morning air. Ahead,

three deer leap the blacktop
like vaporous apparitions
within sight of a derelict barn
collapsing in on itself, making

way for a whole new era, while
cornstalks file past briskly,
going from green to gold,
intent, it appears, on alchemy.

# *Étude for Solo Cello*

*For Dylan Rieck*

Taking up the bow
in his right hand, the cellist
draws it back and forth over the strings
while the digits of his left hand dance,
marionette-like, upon the fingerboard
as though connected to the right
by invisible threads. In this way,
one hand appears to pull the other
along with it in time to the music,
which is tugging at the both of them
by its own unseeable means, leading them
on across measures, through changes
in tempo and dynamics and, ultimately,
with a slight ritardando, to the finish.

## *A Deck of Cards*

Suited as they are
to the sort of abuse
we so often deal out

and well-accustomed
as they must be by now
to all of the shuffling,

riffling and bridging,
the cramped quarters
they have to put up with

there in that slim pack
must seem like nothing,
at least comparatively.

If anything, I'd imagine
such conditions actually
instill a sturdy sense

of fellowship, what with
the royalty commingling
with the peasantry and all.

Further, the rigid nature
of their close confinement
substantiates that old saw

about strength as it relates
to numbers. In any case,
it's only a matter of time

before they wind up back
on the outside, divvied up,
dispersed and duly in hand.

## *Grand Opening*

Driving by the construction site
where the K-Mart was recently razed,

I was startled by the presence
of the exposed foothills beyond,

as though I'd somehow forgotten
they were back there in the first place;

as though I needed reminding
they'll be back there after I'm gone.

## *Listening to Springsteen*

In the last light of evening
I watch the dark water
of *The River* roll past
and then back around again

before lowering the thin straw
of the stylus to drink
from its glistening surface.
Sound spilling from the speakers,

the swirling current sweeps me up,
sailing me from *The Ties That Bind*
to *Hungry Heart,* past *Point Blank*
and clear to *Wreck on the Highway*

prior to plunging me into silence,
the night pooling up around me
as the dark disc of a waxing moon
slips into a papery sleeve of cloud.

## *Flag*

All dim stars
and faded stripes,
Old Glory hangs limp
as a heavy heart
from a bent and rusted pole
outside a rundown farmhouse
on a sepia-toned winter afternoon.
Stirred by the occasional breeze,
its short-lived unfurlings reveal
a tattered state of affairs and the fact
of its being flown upside down,
"a sign that the country is in distress,"
says a passing neighbor. As I watch
his pickup recede from view,
I'm struck by the distance growing
between us, all the more so
with darkness coming on.

## *Creation Story*

My daughter and two classmates
are constructing a diorama
for a high school English project,

taking a world made of words
from a book they had to read
and rendering it in three dimensions

like it wasn't a collection of stories
so much as a set of instructions,
and they weren't ordinary teens

but goddesses, assembling creation
itself in a matter of days, letting there
be an office, a store and a school,

tables, chairs and bookshelves, even
laptop computers and printers, before
deciding their work here is done

and then, presumably, pausing
to look upon all They have made
and see for themselves that it is good.

## *Bicycle in the Snow*

From my upstairs window I can see it
out in the backyard, leaning on the gate,
sugary dollops of fresh accumulation
frosting its red velvet frame. The seat,
pedals and handlebars are amply piled,
as is the hand bell, whose silvery ring
has been muffled here in this wintry hush,
where there's little to chime about anyway
and nowhere, on two wheels at least, to go.

## *Childish Things*

Growing up, my brother and I
collected baseball cards. Not just
of the players of the day, but
vintage ones too, including

such treasured acquisitions
as a 1956 Roberto Clemente,
a 1953 Satchel Paige, and even
a couple dating back to 1909.

By and by, though, our attentions
were pulled in different directions
and our once-unbridled zeal
for the pastime waned, spurring us,

each in our own time, to offload
all but a handful of our favorites,
which we relegated, respectively,
to a desk drawer and a fire safe box,

which is kind of like what we do
with childhood, I guess: tuck it away
somewhere out of the light, and
forget about it for years at a time

until, one day, stumbling on it again,
we find ourselves face to face
with the past, and the parts of us
that are still worth holding on to.

## *Reading in Bed*

Night after night
I open the covers
and slip myself between

the pages of one book
or another, falling back
on pillowy prose or

poetry as I descend,
line by line, into sleep
and, deeper still, into

a vast library of dreams,
where I wander endless
aisles, title upon title

spilling open in my hands
and plots intermingling,
until morning when

I wake to stories strewn
about the sheets, bookmarks
beckoning my return.

## *Dandelions*

As if to emphasize the fact
that spring is now in session,
those perennial standard-bearers
are swarming our front lawn
like the boutonnieres and corsages
that were in such lively abundance
downtown last night, sprouting
from prom dresses, sport coats
and wrists in a collective embrace
of all that is youthful and vibrant,
hope-filled and light, the same
as might even be said of these
taprooted towheads here—quick
to proliferate and, so too, to fade,
going to gray before we know it,
the thin wisps of their dulled blooms
scattering like wishes on the breeze.

## *"Away We Go"*

Out on the edge of West Texas,
nearly to Northern New Mexico,
we passed through a town called Dimmit
that was crumbling into the past.

And there, as I glanced out the window,
I caught sight of the Carlile Theater,
abandoned, or so one would think,
considering the boarded-up windows

and the empty marquee, not to mention
the faded remains of a poster
for a film that I have to assume
was the last to appear on its screen,

and which seemed like a fitting farewell
with a title like the one I made out
there in that fugitive moment
as we sped our way on toward the future.

## *Snow Shuffle*

In the abundant aftermath
of a late February snow,

there's a woman in her driveway
clearing the surface, one arm

in a dark blue sling and the other
steering a shovel, sliding it

and its contents out to the edge
of the inundated concrete,

where, with a nifty little kick
that calls to mind a dance step,

she deposits the load in her yard
before going back for more. Such

is the repetitive, rhythmic footwork
she practices here, she and her fellow

one-armed sashayer, as they move
together in time to whatever music

is urging them on, right up until
the last scrape, which, like a needle

coming off a record, cues their exit
from this makeshift dance floor,

sending them off into the shadows
of the open, waiting garage.

## *Dry Streambed*

You can still feel the presence
of water here, despite the fact
there's nothing left to show for it
but a shallow gully strewn with sand,
rocks and the occasional boulder.
Undaunted, it rushes on, carving
a riverine path right on through
the fertile terrain of my imagination
even as I look out on its absence
and recognize I've arrived too late
to see the last of what might as well
have been the tail of some great beast
lumbering off toward extinction, trailing
this withered waterway like a vestige.

## *At the Botanic Gardens*

Crouching down, my wife
slowly lowers her smartphone
right to the very lip of some
annual, perennial or succulent,
then plants a digital kiss
with a gentle tap of the shutter,
capturing it there in all of its
stunningly transient glory
before moving on to another.

Glancing around, it's clear
that she is anything but alone
in her repetition of this ritual,
what with so many others here
bending before the blooms
in a manner resembling deference
to royalty, cameras extended
outward that the earthly
might be made eternal.

## *The Skull*

My grandparents kept a skull
on a shelf in their apartment
when I was a boy. Not a replica,
mind you, but an actual human skull,
salvaged from my grandmother's days
as a biologist. If that weren't enough,
Grandma put a chicken neck inside
that would rattle when you shook it.
Recalling it now, both grandparents
long in the grave, I'm struck, not just
by their notions of décor, but by the fact
that the end was there in plain sight
the entire time, staring back at us
with hollow eyes, and yet, for me,
it was still little more than a knickknack,
a rattle I didn't know to recognize,
a distant ancestor whose uncertain fate
I'd all too easily learned to live with.

## *Evening Hatch*

In the dissolving twilight
I can see the sky reflected
on the glimmering facade
of this dark ribbon of water,
where, one after another,
trout rise, sending ripples
out to the edge of the cosmos
as they penetrate the surface
of night itself, sipping stars.

## *Dead Air*

After the last song faded
and I was waiting for what came next,

I found myself plunged into a silence
so vast as to seem fathomless,

its cold and mysterious depths
punctuated only by random crackles

of static, with no music or disc jockey
there to help me get my bearings.

And so, untethered as I was
to any of the usual sonic coordinates

and left with no alternatives, at least
none that I could make out there

in that strange and soundless dark,
I did the only thing I could:

took matters into my own hands,
reached out, and turned off the radio.

# About the Author

Michael P. Hill is the author of the chapbooks *Not Just Passing Through* (Main Street Rag Publishing, 2022) and *Junk Drawer* (Kelsay Books, 2021). His poems have also appeared in *Talking River Review, Jelly Bucket, Barstow & Grand, Valparaiso Review,* and *Bricolage,* among others. A near-native of Western Wisconsin, he lives in Northern Colorado with his family.

For more about Michael and his work, visit:
michaelphill.org

www.ingramcontent.com/pod-product-compliance
Lightning Source LLC
Chambersburg PA
CBHW030914170426
43193CB00009BA/847